TOILETS, BATHTUBS, SINKS, AND SEWERS

For my beloved brother
Jonathan Patrick Morgan (1945–1966)
with love forever

TOILETS, BATHTUBS, SINKS, AND SEWERS

A HISTORY OF THE BATHROOM

PENNY COLMAN

Illustrated with Prints and Photographs

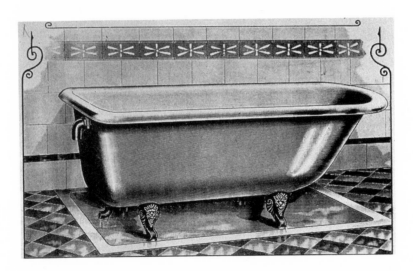

Atheneum 1994 New York

Maxwell Macmillan Canada Toronto

Maxwell Macmillan International

New York Oxford Singapore Sydney

The quotes in the text in the order in which they appear were taken from following secondary sources, which are listed in the bibliography: chapter 1, Mazzurco (1986); chapter 3, Wright (1960); chapter 5, Wright (1960), Mazzurco (1986), Hibbert (1986); chapter 6, Wright (1960); chapter 7, *Plumbing and Mechanical* (1993), *Chicago Daily News* (1939), *Domestic Engineering* (1981).

Atheneum
Macmillan Publishing Company
866 Third Avenue
New York, NY 10022

Maxwell Macmillan Canada, Inc.
1200 Eglinton Avenue East
Suite 200
Don Mills, Ontario M3C 3N1

Macmillan Publishing Company is part of the Maxwell Communication Group of Companies.

First edition   10 9 8 7 6 5 4 3 2 1
Printed in the United States of America
The text of this book is set in Goudy Old Style.

Library of Congress Cataloging-in-Publication Data
Colman, Penny.
   Toilets, bathtubs, sinks, and sewers : a history of the bathroom :
illustrated with prints and photographs / by Penny Colman. — 1st ed.
      p.   cm.   Includes bibliographical references and index.
   ISBN 0-689-31894-4
   1. Bathrooms—History—Juvenile literature. 2. Sanitation—History—
Juvenile literature. 3. Bathing customs—History—Juvenile literature.
[1. Bathrooms—History. 2. Toilets—History.
3. Bathtubs—History. 4. Sanitation—History.]   I. Title.
TH6485.C65 1994   643'.52—dc20   93-48413

SUMMARY:
A history of bathroom facilities from Sumerian and Roman times to the present.

PREFACE

I didn't start thinking about the history of the bathroom until I took a white-water rafting trip down the Colorado River through the Grand Canyon. The trip lasted thirteen days, and it was my first experience of living life without a bathroom. We used river water and biodegradable soap for cleaning ourselves. We spit toothpaste into the fast moving water. We urinated on the wet sand or in the river.

Every night we camped along the river, and the guides set up a toilet for solid wastes behind a boulder or a tree. The toilet was actually a surplus military ammunition can with a toilet seat balanced across the top. A large, green garbage bag was placed inside the ammunition can. In the morning, the guides sealed the bag, lifted it out, carried it to a baggage raft, and placed it in a large metal container that would be carried out of the canyon at the end of the trip. "Don't pee in the toilet or drop in sharp objects," said the guides. "Urine makes it too heavy and you can imagine the mess if a sharp object pokes through the bag."

If we needed a toilet during the day, the guides provided a "day tripper," a small ammunition can with a small plastic bag and no toilet seat. Using it required flexibility, balance, and urgency.

The first and only time I used the "day tripper," I said to myself, "There's got to be a story here!" There was, and here it is: *Toilets, Bathtubs, Sinks, and Sewers: A History of the Bathroom.*

ACKNOWLEDGMENTS

I am particularly grateful to Melissa Kane, Associate Director, Plumbing, Heating, Cooling Information Bureau, Chicago, Illinois, who provided terrific photographs; Lee Allison, The Rowland Company, New York City, who dug extra deep to find just the photographs I needed; and John Laughton, recently retired from American Standard, Piscataway, New Jersey, who graciously responded to my request for information. And also thanks to Heather McCuen, Editor, *Plumbing and Mechanical Magazine*, Des Plaines, Illinois; Emily Teeter, Ph.D., The Oriental Institute, Chicago, Illinois; Laura H. Graedel, Museum of Science and Industry, Chicago, Illinois; Nancy Deptolla, Kohler Company, Kohler, Wisconsin; Christopher Olson, Olsonite Corporation, Detroit, Michigan; Niaz Rasool, Director of Archaeology and Museums, Government of Pakistan; Mary Buchbinder; and my editor Marcia Marshall, who has just the right touch.

As always, I am grateful to my dear friend Linda Hickson and my extraordinarily special sons Jonathan, David, and Stephen Colman.

CONTENTS

1   Splish, Splash, the First Bath   1

2   Seats and Sewers   6

3   The Queen's Toilet   16

4   The Empire's Baths   25

5   Downs and Ups of Sanitation   33

6   Ugh, Gross!   41

7   Lots of Pigs   48

8   Bathrooms Beyond Belief   55

    Ten Facts About Toilets, Bathtubs,
       Sinks, and Sewers   63

    BIBLIOGRAPHY   66
    INDEX   69

TOILETS, BATHTUBS, SINKS, and SEWERS

Children getting clean in a wash basin.

1

Splish, Splash, the First Bath

There is no truer sign of civilization in culture than good sanitation.
A good drain implies as much as a beautiful statue.

J. C. STOBART,
British writer on archaeology

We spend a lot of time in the bathroom. When we need to use the toilet, we go to the bathroom. When we want to clean our body, we go to the bathroom. When we want to brush our teeth, shave, put on makeup, and get cuts and scrapes fixed, we go to the bathroom.

For us, the bathroom is part of our everyday life. It is so common, it is hard to imagine that seventy-five years ago many houses didn't have bathrooms. People used outhouses instead of flush toilets. They poured water from pitchers or buckets into basins instead of using sinks.

It is even harder to imagine that throughout history, there were long periods of time when people rarely bathed. Queen Isabella of Spain, who gave money to Christopher Columbus

1

A young girl brushing her teeth in the bathroom. PHOTOGRAPH BY PENNY COLMAN

for his explorations, was proud that she had taken only two baths in her life.

During these times, people relieved themselves whenever and wherever they had the urge. This was so common that in 1589, the British royal court finally posted a public warning in the palace that read: "Let no one, whoever he may be, before,

2

at, or after meals, early or late, foul the staircase, corridors, or closets with urine or other filth."

The history of the bathroom is fascinating. It starts with our earliest ancestors, who just like us needed to relieve themselves and clean up.

Scientists believe that the first people lived beside water. So, the first bath might have happened when one of our ancestors bent down to get a drink of water and accidentally slipped into a stream. After gasping with surprise and scrambling for safety, the person might have said, "That felt good!" Another person decided to try it. And another. Then someone cleared away branches and big rocks and made the first swimming hole.

To relieve themselves, the first people went whenever they had to and wherever they were. It was a perfectly natural thing to do. After all, everyone did it. Privacy and embarrassment probably weren't things that the earliest humans worried about. They most likely just left their excrement on the ground. Although they might have kicked dirt over it or buried it.

At some point, our first ancestors undoubtedly figured out that water could carry away excrement. It might have happened like this: Imagine a youngster playing in the shallow water of a river. She squats to relieve herself, and an adult standing nearby notices the water carrying the excrement away. Clearly, that looks easier and cleaner than leaving it around the campsite, and soon everyone is using the river as a toilet.

It didn't take long for early humans to realize that it was not very pleasant to drink, wash, and relieve themselves at the same place in the river. Thus, by figuring out that it was better to relieve themselves downstream from where they washed and drank, our ancestors designed the first sanitation system.

Eventually, prehistoric people moved away from the waterside. They left to find more room or better hunting. Now water was usually harder to find, and often it had to be carried from one place to another. Under these circumstances, water was used only for drinking and cooking and not for bathing and waste removal.

Thousands of years passed before ancient people left any signs of having any type of indoor bathroom. Early evidence

A boy from a house lacking an indoor toilet heads for the outhouse to relieve himself. THE BETTMANN ARCHIVES

4

was uncovered by archaeologists during an excavation on the Orkney Islands, a group of islands off the north coast of Scotland. Diggers at the site uncovered a group of huts built of slabs of stone about five thousand years ago.

To get inside the huts, you have to stoop or crawl through a small entrance. Once inside, you discover a bed, dressers, cupboards, and storage space and a hearth with a raised border to contain a fire and ashes. Everything is made out of stone. Along the walls are hollowed out places with a crude drain that led out of the hut to a type of underground sewer system. This meant people didn't have to go outside to relieve themselves. It wasn't much of a bathroom, but it was a start.

Remains of a Neolithic stone hut, which was uncovered in Skara Brae on one of the Orkney Islands off the north coast of Scotland. The hearth is in the center. Not seen in this photo are hollowed-out areas in the wall with a crude drain that served as a type of latrine. The bed, storage area, and dresser were made from stone slabs.
PHOTO BY BILL BUCH-
BINDER

2

Seats and Sewers

By jumping over thousands of miles, we arrive at a region where great farming civilizations were thriving beside mighty rivers. A group of people called the Sumerians grew crops and built cities between the Tigris and Euphrates rivers on land that today is the country of Iraq. In ancient times this land was called Mesopotamia.

The Sumerians learned to mix crushed reeds or straw with river mud and shape it into bricks. Then they let the bricks harden in the sun. Archaeologists have uncovered ancient cities built with these bricks. One of these cities was called Babylon and flourished when Nebuchadnezzar II was king.

Babylon was surrounded by a huge, thick wall. The road that ran along the top of the wall was so wide that chariots could turn around. A broad, straight road paved with stones led through the wall, under eight huge gates, past the royal palaces, and to the main square. A gigantic ziggurat, or temple, stood there. It rose high into the sky and was surrounded by beautiful gardens.

About two hundred thousand people lived in houses crowded along narrow, winding streets made of packed earth. People threw their rubbish and excrement into the narrow streets. When the streets got too messy, people covered the debris with a layer of clay. As this process continued—a layer of filth, then a layer of clay, then filth, then clay—the streets rose higher. Finally people had to build stairs leading *down* from the street to the entrances of their houses until they rebuilt their homes at the new level.

Poor people in Babylon lived in small, round houses made of mud bricks. Wealthy people lived in large houses, many of which had three stories. One good-sized room was set aside for bathing. Here slaves poured water from a jar over the bather. Soap in Babylon was made of ashes and animal fat. Sometimes, instead of using water and soap, people bathed by having a slave anoint, or cover, their bodies with special oils.

The bathroom floor was made of baked bricks. Bitumen, a tarlike substance, was used to make it waterproof. The floor sloped to a drain in the center. Some of the drainpipes were made from a tall jar with the bottom knocked out and inserted in the drain hole.

People who didn't have bathrooms washed in the canals that brought water from the river to the city. Or they bathed in a courtyard where water was stored in cisterns, or tanks.

It seems that there were some privies, a type of toilet house, in Babylon. Most likely the toilet was simply an opening in the floor of a small room or separate building.

An Eastern-style toilet that is in use today. PHOTO BY JONATHAN S. COLMAN

Underneath the opening was a cesspool, a hole in the ground to hold sewage. People would squat over the hole to relieve themselves. This is called an Eastern-style toilet. It is still used today in many parts of the world.

Squatting to relieve yourself may sound strange to people who sit. However, modern scientists say that the ancient people were right—squatting is the best position for defecating. It's more natural and comfortable.

Archaeologists have uncovered other examples of ancient plumbing in other Mesopotamian cities. At Mari, there was a great palace with three hundred rooms, including bathrooms complete with bathtubs. And Sargon II, who ruled years before Nebuchadnezzar, lived in a palace with a Western-style

8

toilet, a toilet with a seat above the cesspool so a person sat instead of squatted. A jar of water with a clay dipper stood beside the latrine. The user poured water from the dipper into the latrine to flush away the waste.

Eight hundred miles to the west, another group of people settled along the Nile River in what today is Egypt. Several million people lived here in ancient times. Most of them were peasants who lived in small houses made of mud. Some Egyptians were very wealthy. Their houses had small bathrooms and lavatories. Since the Egyptians were skilled at making things out of metal, some of the bathrooms had copper alloy pipes that carried hot and cold water.

A stone bath at Tel el Amarna. It has plastered sides and a drain. To the right of the bath is a vase with a hole in the bottom. It is cemented into the earth just below the outlet of the bath and was the original drain. PLUMBING, HEATING, COOLING INFORMATION BUREAU

9

This limestone toilet seat from about 1370 B.C., was discovered in the ancient Egyptian city of Tel el Amarna. It has shaped, smoothed sides. THE EGYPT EXPLORATION SOCIETY

In the ancient city of Tel el Amarna, archaeologists uncovered private houses with bathrooms that had a limestone slab in one corner surrounded by a low wall made of mud bricks. The bricks were covered with stone, which protected them from splashing water. Apparently, a servant stood behind the wall and poured water over the bather, who probably stood on the slab. After running down the bather, the water drained into either a large jar that was later bailed out by hand or through a channel that led through the wall and emptied into a jar outside. Beside the bathroom was a lavatory with a toilet seat placed over a compartment containing sand. Made of wood, terra-cotta (a type of clay), or limestone, the seat was smoothed and shaped with a hole in the middle. Servants cleaned and changed the sand under the toilet seat like people today change kitty litter used by their cats.

Cleanliness was very important to the Egyptians. That was

not just because they wanted to look and smell good, but also because it was part of how they practiced their religion. Ritual bathing, or bathing as part of a religious ceremony, was common throughout Egypt. Ordinary people bathed twice a day. Priests were required to take four cold baths a day.

The Egyptians believed death was not the end of life. They believed that a person who died in this world moved on to life in another world. That is why Egyptians who could afford it were buried in special tombs. All the things that the dead person would need to live in the other world—food, clothing, and furniture—were also buried in the tomb. In some tombs archaeologists have found sink basins. The sinks were carved out of stone and had metal faucets. There was even a lead plug to stop up the drain. The plug was attached with a chain to a bronze ring.

Another great civilization developed to the east along the Indus River in what today is Pakistan. Although the area is

A stone sink with drainboards on each side. It was discovered at the ruins of ancient Thebes, today known as Luxor, Egypt, and is four thousand years old. PLUMBING, HEATING, COOLING INFORMATION BUREAU

Aerial view of a bath and toilet in the Mortuary Temple of Pharaoh Ramses III, who ruled from 1182 to 1151 B.C. It was uncovered at Medinet Habu, a sacred royal center in ancient Egypt. PLUMBING, HEATING, COOLING INFORMATION BUREAU

now mostly desert, thousands of years ago it wasn't. Farmers grew wheat, barley, and cotton. Like the Sumerians, they kept many animals: sheep for wool; pigs, goats, and cattle for food and milk; and water buffalo, elephants, donkeys, and camels to carry heavy loads.

Many villages and small cities spread across the region. Here, about three hundred miles north of the modern city of Karachi, archaeologists have uncovered the ruins of one of the world's first cities. Today, the ruins of this city are called Mohenjo-Daro.

Excavations show it was large and well-organized. Wide, straight streets were divided into regular blocks. Rows of houses made of kiln-dried bricks lined the streets. Because

Sewer drains in the ancient city of Mohenjo-Daro ran between the houses. DE-PARTMENT OF ARCHAEOLOGY AND MUSEUMS, GOVERNMENT OF PAKISTAN

A portion of the sewer drains in the ancient city of Mohenjo-Daro with stone slab covers. DEPARTMENT OF ARCHAEOLOGY AND MUSEUMS, GOVERNMENT OF PAKISTAN

kiln-dried bricks were dried in a big oven instead of the sun, they were harder. Each house looked the same—no windows, low doorway, all the same color. This may sound boring, but Mohenjo-Daro had a most astonishing sewer system and public bath.

Throughout the city, neat, brick-lined sewers ran along the sides of the street. These sewers were connected to each house by an open, brick-lined gutter. Drains inside the house carried kitchen and bathroom wastes out to the gutter. Many houses had one room set aside as a bathroom with a floor of waterproof bricks. In most houses the toilet was Eastern style. However, in several houses, archaeologists have discovered sit-down, Western-style toilets. These toilets had a sloping channel through the wall to a pottery receptacle or brick drain in the street outside.

Mohenjo-Daro's sewer system emptied into a large cesspool. The main cesspool was apparently cleaned out regularly by city workers. All this is quite amazing considering Mohenjo-Daro was built about four thousand years ago.

A great citadel, or fortress, rose on the west side of the city. Important buildings were located within its walls. There was a state granary building where people traded their wheat and barley. A temple sat near the granary. Located between the granary and the temple was the city's most magnificent building—a gigantic public bath.

Just as it was for the Egyptians, bathing was most likely a part of religious ceremonies in Mohenjo-Daro. The bath was built beside the temple so ordinary people and priests could perform the proper rituals.

The bath building stood two stories high. The bathing tank was sunken in a courtyard and surrounded by a covered porch. Everything was made from kiln-dried brick. Water

came from a nearby well. A complicated system of drains was built to empty the bathing tank. People got into the tank by walking down a wide flight of stairs. Around the bath, there were small rooms that might have been changing rooms. In addition there were eight more rooms in two rows along a passageway with a drain. It appears that these private rooms might have been used by the priests.

Far to the west, another civilization was beginning to flourish. There, too, were bathtubs, sinks, and sewers. And an amazing toilet for the queen.

Ruin of the Great Bath at Mohenjo-Daro. It held tons of water. DEPARTMENT OF ARCHAEOLOGY AND MUSEUMS, GOVERNMENT OF PAKISTAN

3

The Queen's Toilet

Now we go to the island of Crete located sixty miles to the southeast of mainland Greece. A peaceable people lived on the island about four thousand years ago. In modern times Sir Arthur Evans, the archaeologist who uncovered palaces on Crete, named these people the Minoans. Sir Evans got the name from a myth that said the first king of Crete was Minos. According to the legend, Minos was the son of Zeus, the supreme god of the ancient Greeks.

The Minoan civilization was the earliest in Europe. Knossos was the capital city where about two hundred thousand people lived. By uncovering the ancient towns and palaces of Crete, archaeologists have learned a lot about the Minoan people. We know from studying fragments of palace

A clay bathtub from about 1700 B.C. that archaeologists found in the Palace of Minos at Knossos. Part of the scrollwork found on the wall in the Queen's Hall has been restored above the bathtub.
MEREDITH PILLON/ GREEK NATIONAL TOURIST ORGANIZATION

A reconstructed wall painting of dolphins found in the Palace of Minos at Knossos, which had toilets, bathtubs, and a sewer system. MEREDITH PILLON/GREEK NATIONAL TOURIST ORGANIZATION

walls that the Minoans decorated them with bright pictures of seaweed, shells, octopuses, dolphins leaping through the waves, and flying fish soaring over the water. Paintings found in the ruins show fashionably dressed men and women. It seems the Minoans liked bright colors and they loved dancing and acrobatics. Young women and men engaged in the sport of leaping onto the backs of running bulls and flipping off. The Minoans also took baths, but apparently not for religious reasons. Instead, they bathed for pleasure.

One of the oldest bathtubs in history was found in the great palace at Knossos on Crete. It doesn't have a drain so it must have been filled and emptied by hand. Even more remarkable was the discovery in the queen's bathroom of a toilet that flushed, the first in history. It had a wooden seat, an earthenware pan, and an elaborate flushing system of pipes and drains that were connected to the sewers.

Water came to the palace at Knossos through pipes made out of terra-cotta. The pipes were tapered and fit snugly together with the narrow end of one pipe set tightly into the broad end of the next pipe. As the water flowed through the narrow end into the broad end, it created a spurting action that washed along debris or sediment and kept the pipes clean. Little handles were made along the sides of the pipes. These were used to tie down the pipes so they wouldn't move around.

Throughout the palace, there were water channels and drains that emptied into huge main sewers under the palace. The main sewers were big enough for a person to walk through.

Suddenly, at the height of its power, the Minoan civilization collapsed. Even today no one is certain what happened. Perhaps there was a great earthquake or an attack by a powerful enemy. Whatever happened, the Minoans' advanced sys-

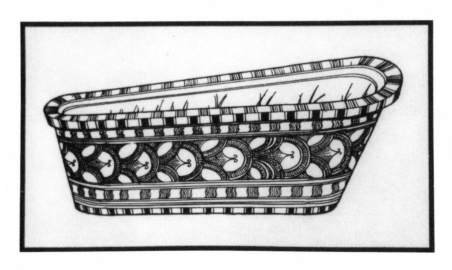

Archaeological reconstruction drawing of the bathtub in the Palace of Minos at Knossos. PLUMBING, HEATING, COOLING INFORMATION BUREAU

tem of running water, drains, and a toilet that flushed was buried.

In nearby Greece, however, another civilization was developing. Like the Minoans, the ancient Greeks also bathed, but not just for pleasure. Many Greeks thought baths were a way to stay physically and mentally healthy—especially nice cold baths. They thought that bathing in warm water made a person weak.

The Greeks did not stretch out in the bathtub. They sat straight up and rested their feet in a part of the tub that was lower. This was the advice given by Hippocrates, an ancient Greek doctor who is called the "Father of Medicine." Hippocrates also believed a cold bath could cure almost any sickness. He advised that "the person who takes the bath should be orderly and reserved in his manner, should do noth-

The Achziv Statuette, a clay artifact of a woman in a bathtub that was buried in the Cemetery ez-Zib, Palestine, at some time between the ninth and the sixth century B.C. It was uncovered by an archaeologist and is now on display in a museum in Jerusalem. It measures 8.3 cm by 10.8 cm. ISRAEL ANTIQUITIES AUTHORITY

ing for himself, but others should pour the water upon him and rub him."

At the ancient city Olynthus, archaeologists discovered bathtubs with drains, probably the first in history. With self-draining bathtubs, the Greeks didn't have to bail out dirty water; they simply removed the plug and the water drained into underground pipes.

The Greeks took outdoor showers by standing under a stream of water coming from a spout. The spouts were found on the sides of large fountains that were built in the cities. Archaeologists have uncovered ancient vases with pictures painted on their sides of people taking showers under fountain spouts.

There were also public bathhouses in Greece, built by the government. These were located near gymnasiums where people did daily exercises. These baths were heated and had warm water. People paid a fee to a bath attendant to use these baths. But they had to watch out for "cloak-strippers," the name for thieves who would steal a bather's clothes. The public baths had rules. One rule was "No singing."

The attendant provided soap, but it was coarse and made from wood ashes and special clay. Many bathers brought their own perfumed soaps, olive oil, and a scraper. The scraper was a curved instrument with a hollow bowl made of bronze. It was used to scrape the bather's skin clean.

Sometimes water was scarce, especially for poor people. So they skipped the water and just cleaned themselves with oil, which they poured on themselves and scraped off.

In addition to public baths, the Greeks had public latrines with toilet facilities that could be used by more than one person at a time. One latrine uncovered by archaeologists had two marble benches with four holes so several people could

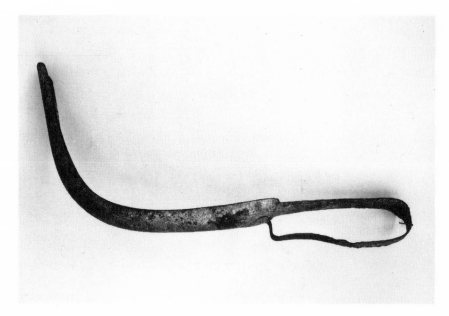

Ancient Greeks used this instrument called a strigil to scrape their skin while bathing. THE METROPOLITAN MUSEUM OF ART, GIFT OF EDWARD ROBINSON, 1911 (11.107)

relieve themselves at the same time. Most likely there was a ditch by their feet with running water to flush away their waste. The latrine had a stone roof and the inside walls were covered with red, yellow, and green plaster.

Many houses had privies that seem to have been flushed by water. These emptied into drains that ran under the streets. Where there were no drains, people would shout, "*Existo,*" "Stand out of the way," and throw garbage and waste into the street. In addition to toilets for adults, the Greeks even had potty chairs for babies to use.

Through the conquests of Philip II of Macedon and his son Alexander the Great, the Greek civilization spread far. Aristotle, a famous Greek teacher, taught Alexander that his soldiers should bury garbage and human and animal excrement far from camp. Similar advice is found in one of the ancient laws of the Hebrew people who lived in Israel. It is recorded in the Bible like this:

You must have a latrine outside the camp, and go out to this; you must have a trowel in your equipment and when you squat outside, you must scrape a hole with it, and turn around and cover up your excrement. For Yahweh your God goes about the inside of your camp to guard you and put your enemies at your mercy. Your camp must therefore be a holy place; Yahweh must not see anything indecent there or he will desert you. (Deuteronomy 23:12–13)

Before he died at a young age, Alexander defeated Darius III and overran that king's mighty empire, the Persian Empire. This vast empire was built by the Iranian people. It stretched from India to Greece and from central Asia to the Nile River.

Archaeologists in Greece uncovered this terra-cotta tub. It is surrounded by clay and stucco. PLUMBING, HEATING, COOLING INFORMATION BUREAU

Zoroastrianism was the national religion of Persia. The Zoroastrian Scriptures, or religious writings, had long sections about cleaning the body and soul. After life itself, cleanliness was considered the greatest act. The Persians were forbidden to eat or drink anything on the street or to spit or blow their nose in public. According to their teachings, even if someone did a good deed, it was worthless if their hands were dirty.

Eventually, the Greeks lost their power, and a people who lived in Rome built an even bigger empire. Today Rome is the largest city in Italy and its capital.

From a small beginning, the Roman Empire grew until it spread throughout Europe, the Middle East, Egypt, and northern Africa. Toilets, sinks, and sewers were an important part of Roman life. So were bathtubs—bathtubs so huge that they were called "the baths."

4

The Empire's Baths

Before looking at the Romans' baths, let us think about the essential ingredient—water.

Throughout history, water has made crops grow, served as roads for ships loaded with goods to trade, and made mills, machines, and factories work. It has also carried away waste and provided baths.

Ancient people got water in a variety of ways. They built canals and ditches to carry river water. They also dug wells. Sometimes, workers had to dig very deep through solid rock to find water. People used large jars to carry water from rivers, canals, or wells. They could also buy it from people called water carriers or water porters, who carried huge jars filled with water throughout the city.

Aqueducts were erected throughout the Roman Empire. This two-tiered section is a bridge, Pont-du-Gard. It was part of a canal that brought the waters of the Airen and Eure springs to Nîmes, a city in the region now known as France. The river can be seen between the trees in the left bottom corner of the picture.
FRENCH GOVERNMENT TOURISM OFFICE

Rainwater was also important. Although some lands didn't get much rain, other areas had a lot. Cisterns, or tanks, were built to catch whatever rain fell.

Aqueducts, large pipes or channels for water, were the most effective way of bringing water long distances to ancient cities. The Babylonians and Egyptians built them underground. The Romans built aqueducts that ran both under and above the ground.

The Romans would locate a source of water such as a mountain spring, where water was coming up from the ground. There they would build a basin to hold the water. From the basin, they would build an aqueduct with channels made of stone or pipes made of lead, earthenware, or stone. Where the land was flat, the channels or pipes ran along the tops of rows and rows of arches for miles and miles. Millions of gallons of water flowed through the pipes to tanks built near the walls of the city. The water from the tanks was used for fountains, public baths, official buildings, private homes, and other purposes.

Because they were able to provide large supplies of water, the Romans created massive public baths. One bath was so big that three thousand people could bathe at the same time!

The public baths were luxurious meeting places. Shops, art galleries, museums, restaurants, libraries, exercise rooms, and lounges surrounded the bathing areas.

Two of the greatest baths in Rome were named after the emperors Caracalla and Diocletian. By examining the ruins of these baths, archaeologists know that they were decorated

A white marble bathtub that was used by Romans from about the fourth to the first century B.C. *It weighs nearly half a ton, stands on a pedestal base, has a rolled edge around the rim, and is about 4 ½ feet long. It doesn't have a drain. Water was poured into the tub and dipped out by hand.* PLUMBING, HEATING, COOLING INFORMATION BUREAU

with beautiful marble, statues, bronze doors, and mosaics—pictures made with small pieces of colored glass, stone, or wood. At a much later point in history, when the bath of Diocletian was no longer being used, the great artist Michelangelo turned it into a magnificent church.

At the beginning of the Roman Empire, people took a bath once every eight days, but as the empire prospered, people bathed every day. Some emperors were said to have bathed seven or eight times a day. The public baths were open from daybreak to 1:00 P.M. for women and from 2:00 P.M. to 8:00 P.M. for men. There were times, too, throughout the history of the Roman Empire when men and women were allowed to bathe together.

An illustration of Emperor Caracalla talking with his architect about plans to expand the baths he provided for the free use of all Roman citizens. Today the Baths of Caracalla are the site of opera performances. THE BETTMANN ARCHIVE

Taking a bath involved several steps. After paying a small fee, bathers undressed and left their clothes in lockers or with an attendant. Just as in Greece, clothes were sometimes stolen. Next, the male bathers generally spent time exercising. They ran on a track, boxed, wrestled, played ball, jumped, or threw a spear or disk. Apparently, no space was provided for women to exercise. They most likely went directly to the tepidarium, or warm-air room, and then the calidarium, or hot-air room, to work up a good sweat. There was a laconicum, or steam room, for bathers who wanted to do serious sweating. Next the bathers took a warm bath. Some hardy bathers then went to the frigidarium, or cold-air room, and plunged into a cold bath. Finally, slaves or attendants rubbed the bathers with oil, scraped their skin clean with curved metal tools called strigils, and dried them with towels. For an additional fee, a bather could have a thorough massage.

Furnaces under the floors of the baths provided heat. Water was heated by running it over hot bricks. Some baths had the ultimate luxury—a bathtub hanging by ropes from the ceiling so the bather could soak and swing.

The Romans bathed for pleasure and good health. Bathing was also a way to socialize—to meet people; do business; talk about politics, love affairs, families, and the weather; and tell the latest jokes.

Rome had a huge underground sewer system called the *cloaca maxima*. The system was built as a drain for rainwater so the streets would not flood. If the water level wasn't too high, a person could travel through it in a rowboat. Parts of it are still being used today.

Public latrines were built throughout the city. These structures were generally erected over a channel of running water. They had stone seats with a hole in the center. A bucket con-

Latrines from the early fourth century B.C. *that archaeologists discovered in a private home in Bulla Regia, a Roman city in northern Africa. The mosaics that are visible on the floor were used on the floors, ceilings, and walls in the houses of wealthy people.* EDITIONS DU SEUIL

taining salt water stood beside each latrine. A long stick with a sponge tied to one end rested in the water. People used the spongy end like toilet paper and then put it back in the water for the next person to use. "Getting hold of the wrong end of the stick" is an expression still used today.

Many people had latrines in their houses, including people who lived on the first floor of brick apartment buildings. Upper-story apartments didn't usually have latrines because it was too hard to install them.

People who didn't have a latrine or didn't want to bother carrying their waste to a cesspool simply threw it out of the window. That was against the law, but they did it anyway.

In the ruins of the ancient Roman city of Pompeii, which was destroyed by a volcano, archaeologists discovered an advanced system of providing running water. Water flowed without stopping through a nozzle in each house. Depending on the size of the nozzle, the homeowner paid a set fee. There were as many as thirty nozzles in some houses.

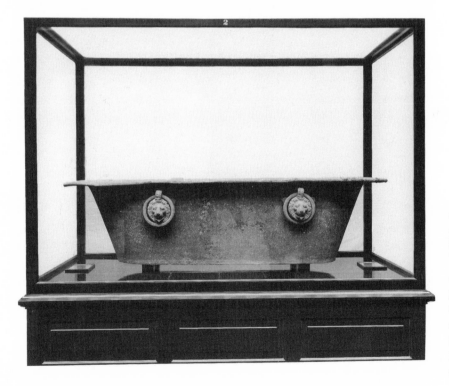

A bronze tub from Pompeii that was buried when Mount Vesuvius erupted in A.D. *79. It is six feet four inches long by two feet deep and on display in a museum.* FIELD MUSEUM OF NATURAL HISTORY #8157

The Romans brought advanced plumbing to every land they conquered. In some places they built baths around hot springs, spots where hot or warm water bubbled up from the ground. One of the most famous was at Bath, England.

Many Roman plumbers were women. The word "plumbing" comes from the Latin word *plumbus*, which means "lead." Throughout history, plumbers have made pipes out of lead because it was easy to bend and didn't rust. Today, plumbers don't use lead pipes because we've learned that lead can cause lead poisoning and brain damage. But for Romans, having lead pipes in their house was a status symbol. It was even more impressive if the plumber stamped his or her name on the pipe, just like brand names on clothes, cars, and shoes today. The Romans also made pipes out of wood and baked clay. Faucet handles were often made in the shapes of animals; dolphins were particularly popular.

Today, you can see ruins of ancient baths in the city of Arles in France, Trier in Germany, Cherchell in Algeria, Ephesus in Turkey, and Bath in England. There are also Roman forts in England with tanks, drains, bathhouses, and latrines. Water from the bathhouses was used to flush the latrines.

For hundreds of years, the Roman Empire was peaceful and prosperous, but in time, the empire crumbled. The final blow was delivered by fierce tribes of people from northern, western, and eastern Europe. For the next thousand years, people in Europe forgot everything that had been learned about toilets, bathtubs, sinks, and sewers.

5

Downs and Ups of Sanitation

The Romans called the warring tribes that overran them from northern, western, and eastern Europe barbarians because they lived in more primitive ways. These invaders had not built great cities or highways like the Romans. Few of them could read or write. And they weren't interested in luxurious baths. In fact, they destroyed many buildings throughout the empire, including aqueducts and public baths. The standard of living declined drastically. Artists, scholars, and builders no longer flourished.

During this time, Christianity, a new religion that had started in the Roman Empire, continued to spread. The beginning of Christianity goes back to the Hebrew, or Jewish, people. The Hebrew people had high standards of hygiene.

Cleanliness was an essential part of their religious practices.

Most early Christian leaders, however, had a different attitude. They thought cleanliness had nothing to do with religion. In fact, bathing was considered sinful. This attitude most likely developed because, near the end of the Roman Empire, public baths had become places for sex orgies and unruly parties.

Saint Benedict, an early religious leader, wrote, "To those who are well, and especially the young, bathing shall seldom be permitted." A later religious leader, Saint Francis of Assisi, listed dirtiness as a sign of a holy person. Saint Catherine of Siena avoided washing. Saint Agnes supposedly died at the age of thirteen without ever having taken a bath.

When bathing was permitted, it was generally a way of doing penance, or washing away evil or bad behavior. Christians also practiced baptism, which involves dipping people in water or sprinkling water over them. Baptism is a sign that a person has become a Christian. One early Christian bragged that after she was baptized, she hadn't washed again for eighteen years! She said she didn't want to wash away the holy water of baptism.

Bathing wasn't totally lost in Christian lands during this time. It was kept alive in monasteries and convents, the buildings where monks and nuns lived. Monks and nuns were men and women who spent all their time studying and practicing Christianity. They took baths two to four times a year for good health and washed their hands and face before every meal. Apparently, monks and nuns felt that bathing would not lead them astray as it would ordinary people, so they indulged themselves. They also had well-kept latrines with a simple system of drains. Old gowns were torn up and used like toilet paper.

Occasionally, wealthy people would take a bath. When they did, the entire family would usually share the same water. That was easier than emptying, filling, and heating the tub over and over again. The tub they used was generally round. Pictures painted during medieval times show people in a tub with a tray of food across the middle of it. Musicians are often shown entertaining the bathers. Nobody seemed to be shy. In fact, some people had their picture painted while they were in the bathtub.

Latrines were found in many castles. They were politely called *garderobes*, or "closets for undressing." Wooden or stone seats were built into the walls. One castle had a four-seated garderobe on each of the three floors. Another had at least twenty seats. The garderobes at Southwell Palace in England were built in a semicircle. Drains under the seats ran outside the castle wall. From the drains, the excrement dropped into a moat, pit, or barrel. Castles also had urinals.

Through history, people have had different names for the toilet. In medieval castles, it was called garderobe, *a word also meaning "wardrobe" or "cloakroom." This drawing shows three garderobes at Southwell Palace that emptied into a central shaft.* CLEAN AND DECENT BY LAWRENCE WRIGHT

Eventually, the excrement from the castle had to be cleaned up. High wages were paid to men willing to do such work. They were called *nightmen* because they worked at night. Excrement was called night soil. Farmers would buy the

In the thirteenth century, a magnificent palace, the Alhambra, was built by the Moors, a people from North Africa who conquered much of Spain and Portugal. This is a view of the Court of Divans, the cooling and resting rooms of the bath. PLUMBING, HEATING, COOLING INFORMATION BUREAU

night soil to use as fertilizer for their crops. Night soil is still used by farmers today, particularly in China.

For hundreds of years, though, most people lived in filth, particularly in European countries like France, England, and Germany. Unlike Mohenjo-Daro and Rome, cities like Paris and London developed without baths, latrines, and sewers. Open ditches were built to carry away rainwater. Unfortunately people also threw garbage and human wastes in the ditches, even though it was against the law.

If people didn't want to bother finding a ditch, they threw debris into the street. According to a journal kept by a person who lived in Paris in the 1700s: "Paris is dreadful. The streets smell so bad that you cannot go out."

Happily, things weren't so bad in other parts of the world. Muslims, the people who practice the Islamic religion, continued to build beautiful baths in the lands they ruled. These lands include what today are Spain, northern Africa, and the Middle East, a larger area than the Roman Empire at its height.

In another great empire, the Ottoman Empire, the Seljuk Turks built elaborate baths with warm rooms, hot rooms, and steam rooms. These were designed for luxury, pleasure, and relaxation.

Marco Polo traveled from Italy to China in the 1200s. He described Kinsai, today called Hangzhou, as "without doubt the finest and most splendid city in the world." According to Polo: "The lay-out is as follows. On one side is a lake of fresh water, very clear. On the other is a huge river, which entering the city by many channels carries away all its refuse and then flows into the lake from which it runs out towards the ocean. This makes the air very wholesome."

Throughout the city there were many public bathhouses.

Rich people had bathrooms in their houses. Twice a day, women and men washed their whole bodies in cold water because it was good for their health. Warm water was available "for strangers who can't bear the shock of the cold."

Marco Polo also observed that the people wiped themselves with their bare left hand after defecating. Then, they carefully cleaned their hand. In India, the Brahmans, elite members of a religious group, also wiped themselves with their left hand. In fact, they considered their house defiled, or made filthy, by the presence of a person who used toilet paper.

Baths were also popular in Japan. Very early in their history, the Japanese had developed the custom of bathing regularly in hot water to clean themselves and relax their bodies and minds. Bathing was part of their religious life.

The Japanese scrubbed and rinsed themselves clean. Then they sat and soaked in a wooden tub filled with hot water. Men and women bathed together in public and private baths without feeling embarrassed, or getting sexually involved with one another. Many Japanese baths were built near medicinal springs, places where water had certain minerals in it. People thought the water was especially healthy for bathing.

The typical Japanese toilet was the hole-in-the-floor kind with a pit underneath. These toilets are still used in many Japanese homes today, although the pits are now regularly emptied by trucks that have suction pumps.

Far across the ocean in what is now Peru, the Incas also had high standards of hygiene. They had sunken baths with stone channels or copper pipes for hot and cold water. Fountains were also made for bathing. Cleanliness was an important part of their religion.

Tenochtitlán, the ancient capital of the Aztecs who lived in what is now Mexico, was a rich city with brick houses,

An ancient bathtub carved out of solid rock at Tezcutzingo mountain, a few miles from present-day Mexico City, Mexico, for Aztec king Netzahualcóyotl. The bath used hot mineral water from a volcano. This photograph was taken in 1939. The people in it were probably members of the archaeological expedition. PLUMBING, HEATING, COOLING INFORMATION BUREAU

canals, palaces, aqueducts, and great buildings. A thousand men worked every day to wash and sweep the city streets. It was said that a person could walk about without worrying about getting dirty feet.

39

The Aztecs bathed often. One way they bathed was to use the *temazcalli,* or "steam bath." This bath is still used in some Mexican villages today.

The temazcalli was a small stone building with a round top and a fireplace on the outside of one wall. The heat from a fire in the fireplace made the wall very hot. The bather crept inside the temazcalli through a low door and threw water on the red-hot wall. This made a cloud of hot steam that surrounded the bather. Then the bather hit his or her body hard with long grasses. Usually, another person would be there to give the bather a massage. Finally, the bather rested on a mat. The bath was used for cleaning the body, as a medical treatment, and as an act of religious purification.

Now let us return to the European countries. How long was it before people started to bathe again?

6

Ugh, Gross!

People in western Europe did start to bathe again, but only after thousands of Christian soldiers, called crusaders, went off to fight the Muslims. Although the crusaders lost the war, they learned about new things during their travels—spices, sugar, intricately woven rugs, and ideas about mathematics and astronomy. They also saw something that had been forgotten in Europe—the bath.

Soon large public baths were common in many European cities. They were called "stews" because people sat in hot water until they felt cooked. After a time, however, people stopped bathing again. There were several reasons for this. As trees were cut down to build houses for more people, it became too expensive to burn wood to heat the water. In addi-

41

A European empire tub from the early nineteenth century that marked the beginning of the trend toward modern bathtubs. It is raised 1 ½ feet off the floor and has a tiny hole in the center for drainage. Lions decorate the tub with their heads under the rim, flowing manes down the legs, and paws as supports. THE SOAP AND DETERGENT AS-SOCIATION

tion, there was a serious increase of diseases and infections, and many people thought the baths were unhealthy. Finally, many baths became places where people bought and sold sex. Just as in Roman times, church leaders forced the baths to close.

Now, few people took regular baths except to treat an illness. These treatments were called water cures, and many doctors prescribed them for their patients.

Special buildings were erected where people could undergo various types of water cures. One cure was called "The Rain Bath for Medical Purposes." The patient stood in a shallow brick pit under a nozzle. When the doctor pulled a cord attached to the nozzle, the patient was drenched with water.

"It is no rare thing to see a subject who at this first shower betrays actual terror, shouts, struggles, runs away, experiences frightening suffocation and palpitations," wrote one person who observed this procedure. Happily, the observer reported that after a few moments, the patient settled down and said, "So, that's all it is."

For hundreds of years, sanitary conditions were terrible, especially in the cities. All the sewage from the millions of people who lived in London emptied into the Thames River. In Paris it emptied into the Seine River. The rivers were thick

Before people had indoor toilets, they used chamber pots. A chamber pot was placed by the bed for use during the night and emptied in the morning. PHOTO BY PENNY COLMAN

In the sixteenth century wealthy people replaced the garderobe with the closestool. This one, which may have been used by Queen Elizabeth I, is covered in crimson velvet. The padded seat has a pot underneath that servants removed and emptied.
CLEAN AND DECENT BY LAWRENCE WRIGHT

with waste, and the smell was horrendous. Even worse than the smell was the fact that people got most of their drinking water from the same rivers. They didn't know that the sewage could pollute the water with invisible germs.

Once in a while, a ruler would try to clean up a city, but money was always a problem. Local citizens refused to pay higher taxes to build sewers. Repeatedly, people said it was easier to get used to the smell and filth than it was to pay more taxes.

In private homes many people relieved themselves in glass urinals or chamber pots. Inexpensive chamber pots were made out of copper or pottery. Fancy ones were made of solid silver. When the pot was full, people emptied it out the window or door into the street. "*Gardez l'eau* (pronounced Garday-loh)," or "Watch out for the water," they would shout, often too late to save a passerby from getting splattered.

Some rich people used closestools, or stools of ease. These were fancy boxes covered with fabric. Each box had a hinged top and a padded seat. A removable pot rested under the seat. Servants would remove the pot and empty it. The French king Louis XIV had 264 closestools at his magnificent palace at Versailles.

Frequently, people would relieve themselves wherever they happened to be. Here is a report of how King Charles II and his court left Oxford, England, after they had paid a visit, "Though they were neat and gay in their apparel, yet they were very nasty and beastly, leaving at their departure their excrements in every corner, in chimneys, studies, colehouses, and cellars."

It was more than one thousand years after the fall of Rome before anything new happened in the history of plumbing. That was when Sir John Harington built the first modern flushing water closet, or toilet, for his godmother Queen Elizabeth I of England. He called it a "privie in perfection." Unfortunately, Harington made the mistake of writing a book with jokes about using his invention. People were disgusted by the book. They mocked Harington and ignored his invention.

As more and more people crowded into the cities, conditions got worse. According to one report written in the 1830s about the city of Leeds in England: "Whole streets were floating with sewage." It took a terrible disease to change people's attitudes.

Cholera, a disease that killed millions of people, had started in Asia. People in western Europe thought cholera would stay away, but it didn't. The disease spread around the world. In 1832 the first cholera epidemic hit London. Thousands of people died. Cholera struck again and again.

At last, an English doctor, Dr. John Snow, proved that drinking water polluted by sewage was the source of the cholera. Finally people learned what today is common knowledge—filthy conditions aren't healthy conditions.

An illustration of workers repairing the Fleet Sewer in London, England, in 1854. HISTORICAL PICTURES

A zinc tub is hidden inside this settee. Used in the late eighteenth century, it was the first tub that didn't have to be hidden because it could pass as a piece of furniture. The top is hinged and it has a chair back with an armrest at one end. The top could be drawn up over the bather like a blanket, and the bather could eat, drink, and entertain people while soaking. It did not have a drain and water had to be poured in and bailed out by hand. THE SOAP DETERGENT AS- SOCIATION

The English government took action. A series of laws were passed requiring houses to have some type of flushing toilet or privy. Money was provided to build a safe sewer system throughout the city. People started to do research on sanitation. Companies made more toilets, sinks, and bathtubs.

Now, in addition to religion, pleasure, physical fitness, social obligation, relaxation, and medical cures, people had another reason to clean up—to stay healthy.

At this point, let us cross the ocean and take a brief look at the history of the bathroom in the United States.

7

Lots of Pigs

Thousands of years before settlers arrived from Europe, Native Americans lived in the area that today is the United States. Their civilization spread from what is now California to Delaware. They had high standards of hygiene. Steam baths, like the temazcalli of the Aztecs, were common. Many steam baths were built partly underground. A tunnel led into the bath.

Unfortunately, the first settlers who came from Europe in the 1600s brought their bad sanitary habits with them.

They rarely bathed except, as in Europe, for medical reasons. In 1799 Elizabeth Drinker, who lived in Philadelphia, Pennsylvania, had a shower bath put up in her backyard for a water cure. After taking her first shower, she wrote in her diary: "I bore it better than I expected, not having been wett all over at once, for 28 years past."

Drinker also wrote in her diary, "My husband went into ye tipid bath. Before dinner, he'd handsel'd [tried out] a new bathing tub which WD [her son William Drinker] bought yesterday for 17 dollars—made of wood, lined with tin and painted—with casters under ye bottom and a brass lock to let out the water."

Many people thought water weakened a healthy person's body. Although a sick person could take a water cure, a healthy person should avoid water. People didn't even like to drink water. A law was passed in Boston in 1845 that forbade taking a bath unless a doctor prescribed it.

The personal tub of the revolutionary war brigadier general Nathaniel Woodhull. It was made of copper and shaped like a violin case. One end has a handle so it could be carried or hung on a peg. Water was poured in by hand and drained out through a small opening in the narrow end. THE SOAP AND DETERGENT ASSOCIATION

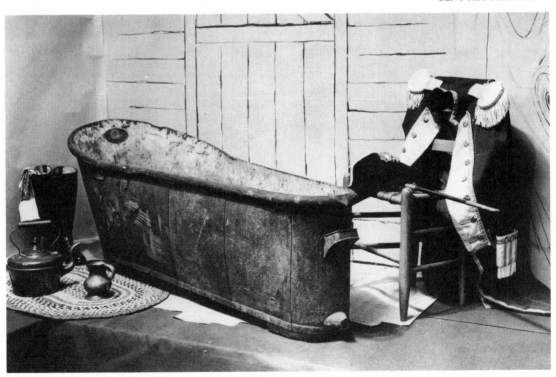

People also avoided bathing because it was too much work. Water had to be carried in a bucket and heated over a fire. The bathtub had to be emptied out with a bucket or hand pump.

One famous early American, however, did recommend bathing—Benjamin Franklin. He particularly recommended the French-slipper bath, a bathtub used by wealthy people in Europe. Franklin discovered the bath when he was the ambassador to France. When he returned to America, he brought a French-slipper bath with him. One of his friends wrote this description of Franklin in his bath: "He sat with his legs under the vamp; on the instep he has a place to fix his book and there he sits and enjoys himself."

The early settlers relieved themselves in forests, used chamber pots and emptied them into the streets, or built outhouses. An outhouse is a little building with a seat with a hole. Many seats had several holes, including a small hole just

A French-slipper bath, the type of bathtub that Benjamin Franklin brought from France to America. It is made of copper. Water was poured in by hand and emptied through a drain in the toe. The opening in the heel is a firebox where a fire was started to heat the water. PLUMBING, HEATING, COOLING INFORMATION BUREAU

50

the right size for a child's fanny. Under the hole was either a deep pit dug in the ground or a bucket.

Children usually had the chore of emptying out the bucket when it was full. That meant lugging the full bucket away from the outhouse, digging a hole in the ground, emptying the waste in the hole, covering the hole with dirt, rinsing out the bucket, and putting the clean bucket back in the outhouse. Outhouses were also called "Necessary Houses," "Handsome Houses," or "Offices." Sometimes people decorated the outside and inside walls of the outhouse with poems and wallpaper. Newspapers or pages torn out of catalogs were used for toilet paper. And for reading.

Towns and cities were built without sewers or septic systems in which sewage drains into an underground tank. The streets were full of excrement, garbage, and pigs. Lots of pigs! People who visited New York City in the 1840s were astonished to see thousands of pigs roaming the streets. Of course, one good thing was the pigs ate up some of the garbage, although even they refused to eat much of what was in the streets. Cincinnati, Ohio, had so many pigs it was nicknamed "Porkopolis." In the southern states, vultures, large, scavenging birds, helped the pigs eat the garbage in the streets.

By the middle of the 1800s, people began to change their ways. Finally they realized that good sanitation was essential for good health. Boston was the first city in the United States to build a system to provide water to its citizens. The pipes were made out of wood. Americans didn't know how to make pipes out of terra-cotta and lead the way the Egyptians, Minoans, and Romans did. Boston also had the first hotel with indoor plumbing. Eight water closets were built on the ground floor near the back of the hotel. Philadelphia was the first city in the world to use cast-iron pipes to carry water to

A Virginian stool shower from about 1830–1840. About 2 ½ feet to 4 feet high, the shower has an attached, wooden soap dish, scrub brush, and revolving seat. A hose ran from a pail of water up the back of the shower and ended above the bather's head or shoulders. By moving the front lever back and forth, the bather pumped water up through the hose. The same motion also moved the scrub brush up and down the bather's back. The water was probably cold. THE SOAP AND DETERGENT ASSOCIATION

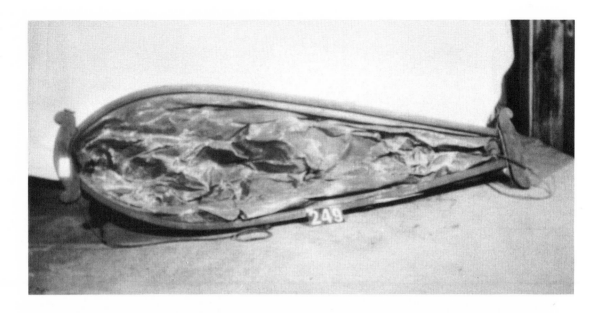

the city. Chicago built the first advanced sewer system.

In 1899 a group of women in New Orleans who were concerned by the inadequate water supply and lack of any sewerage system formed the Women's League for Sewerage and Drainage. At that time, the only women who could vote in New Orleans were women who paid taxes, and they could only vote on tax matters. So, the league decided to force a special election in which taxpaying women could vote to spend tax money to build a new sanitation system. Kate Gordon, president of the league, her sister Jean, and other concerned women prepared a petition and got enough signatures on it to force the special election. The new sanitation system was overwhelmingly approved by female and male taxpayers. In 1919 a bronze plaque was placed on the Sewerage and Water Building (when the building was demolished in 1957, the plaque was removed and placed in a vault in City Hall) that read:

A portable bathtub that was used in the 1880s. The tub held an oilcloth in a wooden frame. The ropes on the ends were used to attach the tub to supports, such as two chairs, posts, or trees. MUSEUM OF SCIENCE AND INDUSTRY

TO THE
ERA (Equal Rights Association) CLUB OF NEW ORLEANS
WHICH ORGANIZED
THE WOMEN'S LEAGUE
for
SEWERAGE AND DRAINAGE
AND THROUGH THE VOTE OF
TAX PAYING WOMEN
HELPED TO SECURE
THE GREAT PUBLIC NECESSITIES OF
WATER, SEWERAGE, AND DRAINAGE

After World War I, American factories started making large numbers of bathtubs, sinks, and toilets. Many indoor bathrooms were built in houses, schools, factories, hospitals, and hotels. Cities and people began to look and smell a lot better.

In 1920 the plumbing industry launched a campaign to promote bathing, bathtubs, and bathrooms. *Domestic Engieering Magazine* published a booklet with illustrations entitled, "The Story of the Bath." Hundreds of thousands of copies were distributed to schools and institutions. Widely read, the booklet undoubtedly created a new consciousness about cleanliness and sold innumerable bathrooms and fixtures. According to the booklet: "Less than 40 years ago [1880], yellow fever and smallpox were frequent callers. And before that, cholera boldly strode the highways and byways counting its victims. Plague spots dotted our landscape. Now all that is changed. And what did it? Pure water piped into the home, poisonous waste piped out of the home. Bathing!" The language is dramatic by today's standards, but the point is still true—proper sanitation is an essential part of life.

8

Bathrooms Beyond Belief

By the mid-1900s, or the middle of the twentieth century, all kinds of bathrooms were being built. Some were large rooms with lots of equipment and decorations. Others were tiny rooms with a water closet and maybe a small sink.

Bathtubs were made for different parts of the body. Bathers could stretch out in a long bathtub. They could sit and soak their hips and buttocks in what was called a sitz bath. They could wash their feet in a footbath, or wash their crotch in a bidet. Toilets were covered with fancy decorations. Sinks were made that stood up on top of a column.

Throughout the 1900s, bathrooms became more common. Today, in some parts of the world, many homes have at least two bathrooms. There are bathrooms with wood-burning fireplaces, bathrooms with exercise equipment, and bathrooms with televisions, VCRs, and the latest equipment for playing music. Some bathrooms have whirlpools, saunas, and steam rooms. Others are decorated with marble, stained glass, silver, gold, and gems. The tubs and sinks come in all different sizes, shapes, and colors.

There are toilets that flush automatically, or if you like, toilets that spray your crotch with warm water, dry you with warm air, and spray on a pleasant scent. When the weather gets cold, the toilet seat heats automatically. In addition, there are toilets that analyze your urine and measure your body temperature, blood pressure, and pulse. Other toilets are designed to use less water or no water. Portable toilets, which are frequently set up at construction sites, outdoor concerts, or fairs, use chemicals to cut down odor and need to be emptied after use.

A bathroom in Fort Madison, Iowa, probably in the late 1890s. A hot-water heater with a hose hanging down is above the tub. The privy is flushed with the hose that is attached to the cold-water pipe.
CRANE NEWS

In 1991 an American company advertised this as the "Fantasy Bath."
Designed around an Arabian Nights theme "to suggest luxury and seclusion,
key elements in today's dream bathroom." A whirlpool bath is in the fore-
ground. KOHLER COMPANY

If Kathie Kidder Jones is right, this female urinal that she designed, the She-inal, will become a standard fixture in women's public bathrooms. PHOTOGRAPH COURTESY OF URINETTE, INC., PENSACOLA, FLORIDA.

There are even toilets for outer space. Actually the first astronauts used plastic bags. The bags had sticky strips so they would stick to the astronaut's body. Urine went in one bag and excrement in another. The astronauts freeze dried their excrement so scientists could analyze it after their voyage.

Later astronauts who flew on the shuttle had a toilet. It even had curtains for privacy. Skylab I and II had showers.

Back on earth, there are showers designed for people in wheelchairs, showers with fold-down seats, showers with two or more nozzles so people can shower together, and showers that use steam instead of water. There are "touchless faucets"—just stick your hands under the spigot and the water starts running—and "flushless toilets"—just stand up and the toilet flushes.

Even computers have come to the bathroom. One feature, called auto-fill, lets you program your bathtub or whirlpool to fill up with water at any time and temperature you desire. In 1993 a gasoline company started experimenting by installing computerized, self-cleaning bathrooms in several gas stations. The station attendant presses a button to activate thirty-nine

AD 2000
COMFORT CONTROL CENTER by OLSONITE

This toilet seat, The A.D. 2000 Comfort Control Center, was designed and built in the 1960s. It features a stereo sound system, heating element, reading light, and an armrest that folds up when not in use. It was never actually produced for consumers, but was certainly made for a bathroom beyond belief. OLSONITE CORPORATION

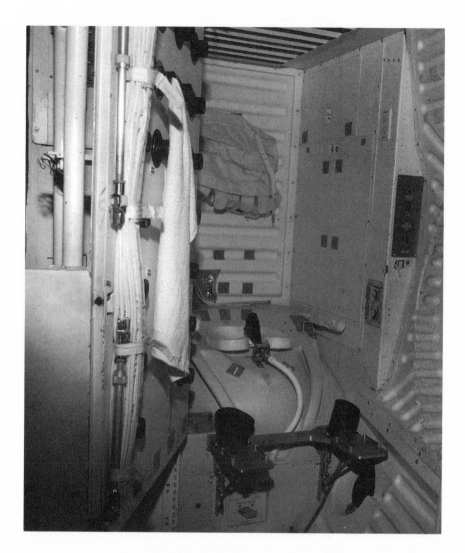

The original waste system on the space shuttle. NATIONAL AERONAUTICS AND SPACE ADMINISTRATION

nozzles that spray cleanser and water on the walls and fixtures. Warm air then dries the room. The bathroom is spotless in twenty-four minutes.

Despite all these advances, there are still areas in the world, including the United States, where people don't have running water and bathrooms. Some areas are too poor. Some areas have very little water. We can hope that at this point in

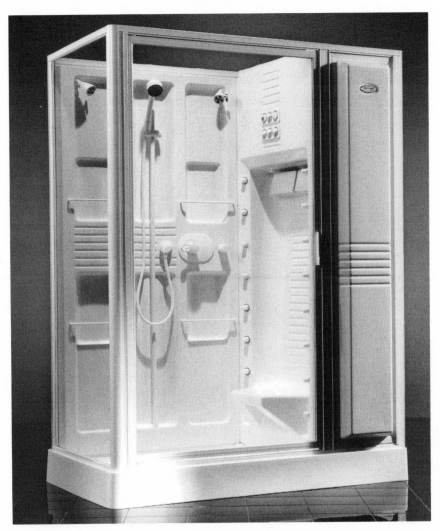

According to the manufacturer, this J-Dream is the "ideal replacement for a traditional bathtub" in the 1990s. It has sixteen whirlpool jets, two fixed shower heads, one hand-held shower head, a seat under a waterfall, a steam bath, and a built-in closet that warms towels and robes. THE J-DREAM BY JACUZZI WHIRLPOOL BATH

the history of the bathroom, good sanitation will soon be available for all people, and everyone will have access to a bathroom—a room for defecating and urinating, for cleaning and preening, for reading a book, and for being alone. After all, the bathroom has been around for thousands and thousands of years.

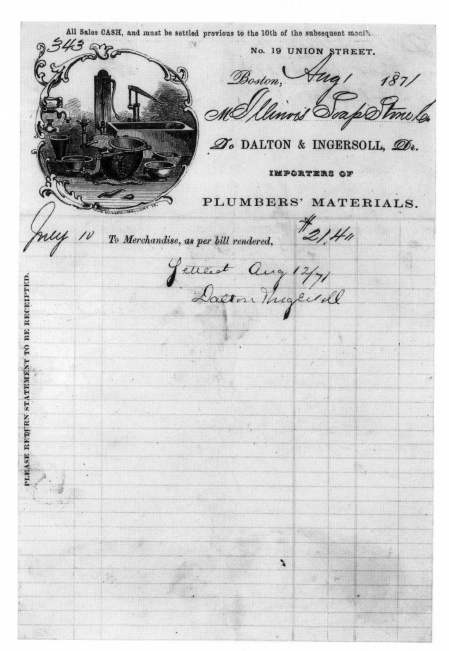

All Sales CASH, and must be settled previous to the 10th of the subsequent month.

No. 19 UNION STREET.

Boston, *Aug 1* 1871

Mc'Illinois Soap Stove Co.

To DALTON & INGERSOLL, Dr.

IMPORTERS OF

PLUMBERS' MATERIALS.

July 10 To Merchandise, as per bill rendered, #21,41

Settled Aug 12/71
Dalton Ingersoll

PLEASE RETURN STATEMENT TO BE RECEIPTED.

A bill dated 1871 from Dalton & Ingersoll, a company that imported plumbers' materials to sell in the United States. The logo in the upper left-hand corner shows some of the plumbers' materials.
SMITHSONIAN INSTITUTION

Ten Facts About Toilets, Bathtubs, Sinks, and Sewers

1. The common belief that Thomas Crapper invented the toilet is not true. Born in 1836, Crapper was a successful plumber in England and received nine patents for plumbing related products. However, Crapper's patents are not for the toilet used today. In fact, in 1775, Alexander Cummings received the first patent for a forerunner of the toilet used today. In 1778 Joseph Bramah received a patent for an improved version.

2. According to a study, the majority of people stand up before they flush the toilet.

3. The Japan Toilet Association (JTA) was established in 1985, the first organization in the world "entirely committed to the toilet." According to JTA, "Despite the fact that the toilet is an indispensable feature in daily life, it is obvious the toilet is still held in relatively low regard in our social consciousness." JTA aims to create a "toilet culture," a new area of human activity and information based on research and discussions about public restrooms throughout the world. The France Toilet Association was formed in 1989. In 1993 an International Toilet Symposium was held in Japan with speakers from the United States, Australia, France, Korea, China, Hong Kong, and Thailand.

4. According to a survey, Americans average about eleven minutes in the shower and about twenty minutes in a bath.

5. In 1895 George Washington Vanderbilt had a mansion built in Asheville, North Carolina. It had 57 bathrooms. There was a huge, round tub in Vanderbilt's personal bathroom. Mrs. Vanderbilt's bathroom had a bathtub and shower. However, instead of a sink, there was a washbowl and pitcher with the family insignia stamped in gold on a slab of marble.

6. In 1908 a hotel in Buffalo, New York, advertised, "A Room and a Bath for a Dollar and a Half."

7. In 1927, for the first time, bathtubs, toilets, and sinks were available in colors. In addition to the standard bright white, consumers could choose from spring green, lavender, autumn brown, old ivory, and horizon blue.

8. In 1993 reports estimated that there are about 200,000 bath injuries a year, including burns from hot tap water and falls.

9. Many underground sewers and water pipelines in use in the United States in the 1990s were installed over one hundred years ago, and they are in poor condition. According to a report, leaky pipes cause some major cities to lose as much as 30 percent of their fresh water supply each day.

10. Americans alone flush 4.8 billion gallons of water a day. Beginning January 1, 1994, water-saving toilets that use only 1.6 gallons of water per flush are required by federal law in all new installations. Up to now, most toilets have used 3.5 gallons per flush. If all toilets in the United States were replaced with low consumption 1.6-gallon-per-flush toilets, only 1.54 billion gallons of water would be consumed daily, representing a 68 percent savings.

This old sitz bath came from Germany.
PHOTO BY PENNY COLMAN

BIBLIOGRAPHY

"America's First 200 Years: Not Much to Be Said for Sanitation."
Domestic Engineering (October 1981): 30, 34.

Aries, Philippe, and Georges Duby, eds. *A History of Private Lives.*
Cambridge, Mass.: Belknap Press of Harvard University, 1987.

Auboyer, Jeannine. *Daily Life in Ancient India: From Approximately
200 B.C. to 700 A.D.* New York: Macmillan Co., 1965.

Barlow, Ronald S. *The Vanished American Outhouse: A History of
Country Plumbing.* El Cajon, Calif.: Windmill Publishing Co.,
1989.

Bibby, Geoffrey. *Four Thousand Years Ago: A World Panorama of Life
in the Second Millennium B.C.* New York: Alfred A. Knopf, 1963.

Braudel, Fernand. *The Structures of Everyday Life.* Vol. 1, *The Limits
of the Possible.* New York: Harper and Row, 1979.

Cottrell, Leonard. *The Mystery of Minoan Civilization.* New York:
World Publishing Co., 1971.

De Camp, L. Sprague. *The Ancient Engineers*. Garden City, N.Y.: Doubleday and Co., 1963.

De Mente, Boye. *Passport's Japan Almanac*. Lincolnwood, Ill.: Passport Books, 1987.

Derry, T. K., and Trevor I. Williams. *A Short History of Technology: From the Earliest Times to A.D. 1900*. New York: Oxford University Press, 1961.

Durant, Will. *The Story of Civilization*. Part 1, *Our Oriental Heritage*. New York: Simon and Schuster, 1935.

——. *The Story of Civilization*. Part 2, *The Life of Greece*. New York: Simon and Schuster, 1935.

"Firm Cleaning Up Data on Bathtubs in America." *Chicago Daily News* (March 25, 1939): 22.

Fisher, Charles E., III, ed. *The Well-Appointed Bath: Authentic Plans and Fixtures from the Early 1900s*. Washington, D.C.: Preservation Press, 1989.

Furnas, J. C. *The Americans: A Social History of the United States, 1587–1914*. New York: G. P. Putnam's Sons, 1969.

Garrett, Elisabeth Donaghy. *At Home: The American Family 1750–1870*. New York: Harry N. Abrams, 1989.

Graham, James Walter, et al. *The Palaces of Crete*. Princeton, N.J.: Princeton University Press, 1977.

Green, Harvey. *The Uncertainty of Everyday Life, 1915–1945*. New York: HarperCollins, 1992.

Hamblin, Dora Jane. *The First Cities*. New York: Time-Life Books, 1973.

Hibbert, Christopher. *Cities and Civilizations*. New York: Weidenfeld and Nicolson, 1986.

"The History of Plumbing, Parts 1–8." *Plumbing & Mechanical Magazine* 10 (June 1993): 6–124.

Johnston, Mary. *Roman Life*. Glenview, Ill.: Scott, Foresman and Co., 1957.

Kamil, Jill. *The Ancient Egyptians: A Popular Introduction to Life in the Pyramid Age*. New York: Columbia University Press, 1977.

Kendall, Ann. *Everyday Life of the Incas*. London: B. T. Batsford, 1973.

Kira, Alexander. *The Bathroom Criteria for Design*. Ithaca, N.Y.: Cornell University Press, 1966.

Lindsay, Jack. *The Ancient World: Manners and Morals*. New York: G. P. Putnam's Sons, 1968.

Mazzurco, Philip. *Bath Design: Concepts, Ideas, and Projects*. New York: Whitney Library of Design, 1986.

Palmer, Roy. *The Water Closet: A New History*. London: David and Charles Publishers, 1973.

Saggs, H. W. F. *The Greatness That Was Babylon*. New York: Hawthorn Books, 1962.

Sherr, Lyn, and Jurate Kazickas. *The American Woman's Gazetteer*. New York: Bantam Books, 1976.

Stobart, J. C. *The Grandeur That Was Rome*. 4th ed. New York: Hawthorn Books, 1961.

"The Story of the Bath." *Domestic Engineering* (October 1981): 166–167.

Stuller, Jay. "Cleanliness Has Only Recently Become a Virtue." *Smithsonian Magazine* 21 (February 1991): 126–134.

Sutherland, Daniel E. *The Expansion of Everyday Life*. New York: Harper and Row, 1989.

Thomas, Hugh. *A History of the World*. New York: Harper and Row, 1979.

Tucker, T. G. *Life in Ancient Athens*. New York: Macmillan, 1936.

Von Furstenberg, Diane. *The Bath*. New York: Random House, 1993.

Wright, Lawrence. *Clean and Decent: The Fascinating History of the Bathroom and the Water Closet, and of Sundry Habits, Fashions and Accessories of the Toilet, Principally in Great Britain, France, and America*. New York: Viking Press, 1960.

INDEX

Note: Page numbers in italics refer to illustrations.

A.D. 2000 Comfort Center, 59
Aqueducts, 26, 26–27, 38–39
Aristotle, 22
Aztecs, 38–40

Babylon, 6–8, 26
Baptism, 34
Barbarians, 32–33
Bathrooms, 1, 54, 55, 59, 60
  fanciness of, 55–56, 56, 57
  in homes, 4–5, 5, 9, 14, 38
Baths, 3, 9, 32, 64, 65. See also
    Public baths
  frequency of, 1–2, 11, 28, 40
  for health, 20, 29, 34, 38,
    47, 48–49
  for pleasure, 18, 29, 34, 37
  reasons for, 34, 38, 40
  reasons to avoid, 41–42,
    49–50
  ritual, 11, 14–15, 38
  by servants, 7, 10, 20–21
Baths of Caracalla, 27–28, 28
Bathtubs, 12, 19, 35, 42, 47,
    53, 55, 61. See also
    Drains

materials for, 17, 23, 31, 39,
    49, 49, 50
  Roman, 27, 29
  sitting in, 20, 20
Bible, the, 22–23
Bidet, 55
Bramah, Joseph, 63
Bricks, 6–7, 10, 12–14

Canals, 7, 25, 38–39
Cesspools, 8, 14, 31, 38
Chamber pots, 43, 45, 50
China, 37–38
Cholera epidemic, 46
Christianity, 33–34
Cisterns, 7, 26–27
Clay, 17, 32
Cleanliness, 10–11, 54
  teachings on, 22–23, 24
Closestool, 44, 45
Cloth, as toilet paper, 34
Clothes thieves, 21, 28
Computers, 59–60
Copper, 38, 49, 50
Crusades, 41
Cummings, Alexander, 63

Ditches, 25, 37
Drains, 7, 10, 22, 35

for bathtubs, 18, 21, 27, 47

Eastern-style toilets, 8, 8
Egypt, 9–11, 26
England, 46
Excrement, 3, 22–23, 36–37,
    51, 58
Exercise, 21, 29

"Fantasy Bath," 57
Fountains, 21, 38
Franklin, Benjamin, 50
French-slipper tubs, 50

Gordon, Kate, 53
Governments, 45, 47
Greece, 20–23

Hands, used for wiping, 38
Harington, Sir John, 45–46
Health, 38, 42–43
  baths for, 20, 29, 34, 38
  sanitation for, 44–45,46–47,
    51, 54
Hippocrates, 20–21

India, 38

Japan, 38, 64

"J-Dream," 61
Jewish people, 22–23, 33
Jokes, 45–46

Latrines, 30–31, 34
    in castles, 35, 35
    public, 21–22, 29–30, 30
Lead pipes, 32

Marble bathtubs, 27
Massage, 29, 40
Mesopotamia, 6–9
Metal, 9, 11, 31
Minoans, 16–20
Mohenjo-Daro, 11–15
Muslims, 37

Native Americans, 48
Night soil, 36–37

Oils, bathing with, 7, 21
Orkney Islands, 4–5
Ottoman Empire, 37
Outhouses, 4, 50–51

Pakistan, 11–15
Palaces, 2–3, 38–39, 45
Persian Empire, 23–24
Pigs, in cities, 51
Pipes, 26–27, 32, 65
    materials for, 9, 19, 38, 51
Plumbers, 32
Polo, Marco, 37–38
Potty chairs, 22
Privacy, 3, 35
Privies, 7–8, 22
Public baths
    in China, 37
    Europe, 41–42
    in Greece, 21

in Mohenjo-Daro, 14–15, 15
    Roman, 27–29

Religion
    baths in, 38, 40
    cleanliness in, 10–11,14–15,
        22–24, 33–34
Rivers, as sewers, 3, 37, 43–45
Rome, 24, 25–32

Sanitation, 22–23, 60–61
    of cities, 7, 14, 43–45,
        46–47, 51–54
Scrapers, for baths, 21, 22, 29
Self-cleaning bathrooms,
    59–60
Sewers, 46
    ancient, 5, 13, 14, 18–19, 29
    modern, 51, 53–54, 65
    rivers as, 3, 37, 43–45
Sex, and baths, 34, 38, 42
Showers, 21, 42–43, 48–49, 52,
    59, 64
Singing, forbidden, 21
Sinks, 2, 11, 11
Sitz baths, 55, 65
Slaves, 7, 10
Smell, 37, 44
Snow, John, 46
Soap, 7, 21
Space, bathrooms in, 58–59, 60
Squatting, 8
Steam baths, 48
Steam rooms, 29, 37, 40
"Stews," 41–42
Stool shower, 52
Streets
    cleanness, 38–39
    filth in, 7, 22, 31, 37,45
Strigils, for baths, 21, 22

Taxes, 45, 47
Temazcalli (steam bath), 40
Toilet paper, 29–30, 34, 38, 51
Toilets, 14
    closestool, 44, 45
    flush, 18–19, 45–46
    inventors of, 63
    in Japan, 38
    in Mohenjo-Daro, 12
    options on, 56, 59
    privies, 7–8
    sand, 10
    seats on, 8– 9, 10
    in space, 58–59
    water-saving, 56, 65

United States, 48–54
Urinals, 35, 58

Vultures, 51

Water, 3
    drinking, 3–4, 44, 46
    running, 22, 31
    shortages of, 21, 60
    for toilets, 18–19
    transportation of, 4, 25–27
    wasted, 65
Water cures, 42–43, 48–49
Water systems
    ancient, 9, 19, 26–27, 31–32
    modern, 51, 53, 65
Water-saving toilets, 56, 65
Wells, 25
Women's League for Sewerage
    and Drainage, 53–54
Wood, 32, 49, 51

Zoroastrianism, 24